MW01716434

Persiansk

Poems of Spiritual Awakening, Identity, Exile, and Inner Wisdom

by

Ramin Taheri

Words from Early Readers of *Persiansk*

"Persiansk is a profound and personal collection rooted in self-reflection, spirituality, and life itself. Ramin has a rare gift for playing with language—his words interweave like contrasts and gateways to wisdom and insight. It's a pleasure to read, a balm for the soul. This is not lofty pseudo-poetry, but a heartfelt celebration of language and life, written in a voice anyone can understand. I was especially moved by Let it Go, Surrender, and Unity, as well as the entire Nowruz section and the reflective Poetic Meditation Verses."

– ARC reviewer (translated from Danish)

"Poetry is slowly circling its way back to me — and this collection played a big part in that. The poems are beautifully written, simple yet profound, and easy to connect with. Each piece holds hidden gems that encourage self-reflection and emotional clarity.

This is one of the most beautiful poetry collections I've read in a long time. It's the kind of book you'll keep returning to

— for comfort, insight, and peace. I'm honored to have read it."

— ARC Reviewer

"A beautiful experience!
Ramin's poems invite the reader on a personal journey —
from Iran to Denmark, from youth to reflection.
His language flows effortlessly,
evoking life's paradoxes with gentle power.
Even joy carries a quiet melancholy. I was especially touched by 'Mommy, No More Books Please.'"

– ARC Reviewer (translated from Danish)

From the very first poem, I felt like I was receiving a comforting yet intense embrace. The rhythm made me read out loud, and the words made me stop and reflect—on where I am in life and what truly matters. "Mommy, No More Books Please" and "Moved to Denmark" were especially profound; I felt like a small piece of the writer's soul had been shared with me.

– ARC Reviewer

Published by: Persiansk Press
ISBN: 9788797623909
Illustrations and cover design by: Aimeé Cervantes Flores

To my wife—whose quiet strength and love are the foundation of every word I write.

To my daughter—whose wonder and laughter open doors within me I never knew existed.

To the poets who came before me—your words lit the path I now walk.

And to you, dear reader—your presence gave me the courage to keep writing.

Preface

Persiansk is a journey through inner landscapes, a meditation on the soul's restless dialogue with the world. These poems span over a decade of transformation—of exile and homecoming, silence and speech, faith and doubt. Each verse carries a moment lived, a truth discovered, or a wound endured. Some poems rise like whispered prayers. Others speak boldly, burning with the fire of inquiry and pain.

This collection was not written with performance in mind, but with presence. These are not merely poetic expressions—they are meditations, offerings, and sometimes confessions. Born in moments of heartbreak and healing, in faraway cities and familiar silences, they reflect a life lived between cultures, geographies, and spiritual traditions.

The name *Persiansk* itself is a merging of identities—a symbolic fusion of the Persian soul with Nordic clarity. It is a testament to the immigrant's balancing act: between rootedness and reinvention, memory and momentum. The collection holds reflections from this in-between space, where longing meets resilience and tradition walks beside change.

Each poem serves as both mirror and window: a mirror into the self, and a window into the shared human experience. From the ache of separation in *Tomorrow Without You*, to the resilience woven into *The Power of Silence*, from the spiritual depth of *Surrender* to the mythic reverberations in *No Rest*, the collection pulses with the tensions between the divine and the human, between struggle and surrender.

There is rhythm in these tensions—an emotional heartbeat that flows like a river across the chapters. The journey begins with raw questions: *Who am I? What does it mean to belong?* And as it unfolds, there is a shift into stillness and clarity, where insight arises not from answers but from presence.

Some of these chapters are tied to the rhythms of the Persian calendar, particularly the celebration of Nowruz—the Persian New Year. In these sections, you'll find poems dated according to the Solar Hijri calendar (e.g., Nowruz 1402, 1403). For reference, Nowruz 1402 corresponds to spring 2023 in the Gregorian calendar. These markings were kept to honor the cultural and seasonal spirit that shaped their writing.

Astrology has also whispered its influence across these pages. In several poems, constellations and planetary forces emerge—not as rigid beliefs, but as poetic metaphors that reflect the hidden architecture of our inner lives. The stars become symbols of change, destiny, and cosmic rhythm, suggesting that perhaps we are not entirely separate from the sky's design.

One of the guiding principles of this book is a deep philosophical openness: a willingness to question everything—and to welcome all possible answers. I do not write from a place of certainty, but from the understanding that truth is rarely absolute. What feels wrong in one moment may be right in another. What we call "true" or "false" is often shaped by time, place, and perception. In this light, right and wrong begin to dissolve into something more human, more fluid.

Everyone's reality holds its own integrity—and perhaps, in their own way, everyone is right. These poems do not aim to resolve such paradoxes, but to give them room to breathe. To invite you, too, to dwell in the questions.

Migration, identity, and spiritual longing are ever-present undercurrents. Poems like *Moved to Denmark* and *Copenhagen Dream* illuminate not just the external dislocation of the immigrant, but also the internal recalibration required to survive and grow in unfamiliar soil. These are not romanticized tales, but honest explorations of labor, disillusionment, quiet dignity, and hard-earned hope.

Nature, too, breathes throughout these pages. The wind, the sea, the sun, and the silence between storms—these are not just metaphors but companions. They witness the poet's unraveling and reassembly. In poems like *A Spring in Norway* and *Close Your Eyes, Look Within*, the natural world becomes a spiritual guide, reminding us to slow down, to listen deeply.

Above all, this book is about connection. Between

people, between the soul and the divine, between the poet and the reader. In the wisdom of a father, the sorrow of a mother, or the silent question of a wandering son—love reveals itself, not always gently, but always with purpose.

These poems do not promise resolution. They are not final answers. But they open space—space for reflection, for stillness, for recognition. They are here to accompany the seeker, the grieving, the curious, and the hopeful. They are here to remind us: even in darkness, there is light. Even in brokenness, there is grace.

Welcome to *Persiansk*. May it find you exactly where you are—and walk beside you, long after the final page is turned.

— **Ramin Taheri**

Copenhagen, 2025

Introduction

Persiansk is a collection of poems born from years of migration, inner search, and spiritual longing. Rooted in my journey from Iran to Denmark, the poems reflect personal struggles and shared human experiences—love, loss, healing, and faith.

The title *Persiansk* blends "Persian" with "dansk" (Danish), symbolizing the meeting point of two cultures and two spiritual traditions: Persian mysticism and old Norse wisdom. The poems live in that in-between space, where heritage meets renewal, and where memory speaks alongside hope.

These poems are for anyone navigating complexity—between cultures, beliefs, or moments of change. I hope they offer presence, peace, and a reminder that even the most personal stories can speak universally.

Table of Content

I. Self-Exploration and Identity

Who Am I?

Who am I,
Trapped in the wheel of life?
Grasping daily desires,
Hoping pain will subside.
Between the climbs
To the conscious peak,
I fall to the nadir—
My mind grows weak.
Who would I be
If my parents weren't here?
Sarcastically,
Another "I" would appear.
As we all are called,
Bound by the vow
To live as "selves,"
Yet question it now.
The core of all beguilement
Must be unveiled,

Once consciousness frees itself

From the wheel derailed.

The world is planned—

As above, so below—

This will rise,

That will fall,

While others bestow.

Now is the time;

The wheel spins anew.

The Archer plays the devil,

Horses in view.

Taurus reigns on the throne with might;

Scorpio leads, embracing the night.

This Zodiac sets the course of the whole—

Barbs in the eyes,

The cost of control.

To perceive the world

As it truly is

Demands a price—

Beneath, a hidden abyss.

Mommy, No More Books Please

Once upon a time,
I was just a child,
Lost in books,
Where my mind ran wild.

Mom would buy them,
Stack them high,
To keep us busy,
To let time fly.

She thought it a favor,
A harmless deed,
Leaving us pages
To learn and read.

Little did she know,
With each book we turned,
A fire of wisdom
Quietly burned.

The more we read,
The more we grew—
A blessing at first,
But a curse, who knew?

For knowledge, unchained,
Is a lonely road,
A weight too heavy,
A mind that glowed.

Mom believed
The books would teach us well,
But wisdom resists
Where ignorance dwells.

It questions, it seeks,
It stands alone,
Unwelcome in places
Where power is throne.

Years went by,
And we faced rejection—

Not for our faults,
But for our perception.

We read the rules
Between the lines,
Saw the flaws
And the hidden signs.

For wisdom stings,
It shakes, it breaks,
It rattles the world,
It wakes mistakes.

Yet instead of seeking,
They turn away,
Afraid to listen,
Scared to stay.

The more we sought,
The more we fell—
Truths uncovered,
Yet none to tell.

In a world of noise and cheer,

A silent thinker sparks their fear.

My mother did

The best she knew,

Gave us books,

Let wisdom brew.

Yet never foresaw

How high we'd climb,

Or how alone

We'd stand in time.

Perhaps it's best
To stay at bay,
To let deep thoughts
Just drift away.

For children now,
I make my vow:
No sacred books,
No furrowed brow.

One last word I have,
To those who see:
If you seek truth,
Then gently let it be.

Either live in bliss,
Unscarred, undone,
Or stand alone—
For you'll be The one.

Judgmental Me

You feel their eyes,
Their whispers near,
A stage is set
In daily fear.

But truth be told,
They rarely see,
Not nearly as much
As you believe them to be.

A number first,
A thought aligned,
Shapes decisions,
Traps the mind.

Random weights
We treat as true,
Yet bias clouds
The clearer view.

It cannot switch off,
Nor disappear,
But know its grip—
Stay sharp, stay clear.

What anchors first
Will set the tone,
A tale is shaped,
Its seeds are sown.

The first impression
Lingers long,
The early call,
The loudest song.

We chase a force
To even fate,
Yet chaos laughs—
It will not wait.

No unseen hand
Will make things fair,

Events unfold
Without a care.

Absolute truth
Is hard to find,
Sharp contrast fools
The human mind.

We weigh the world
In biased light,
While randomness
Escapes our sight.

Seek and find
What you expect,
The world conspires,
Thoughts connect.

A tunnel vision,
False yet sweet—
Avoid its trap,
Don't be deceived.

Turn the page,
Search anew,
Challenge all
You thought you knew.

Step beyond
The gambler's glance,
Don't let fate
Decide by chance.

A task half-done,
A thought laid bare,
Your mind insists
It must repair.

Patterns form
Where none exist,
A longing pull,
A clenched-up fist.

The choice you make,
The road ahead—

Will paradox

Still paint it red?

Completion lures,

But step with care—

Not all endings

Are truly there.

I. Self Exploration and Identity

II. Wisdom and Guidance

A Father's Advice

Ramin, don't make life too hard,
Let it flow, soft and unmarred.

In God's grace and mercy wide,
All will settle, none to hide.

Be grateful for the gifts you know,
Greater things will surely grow.

Don't chase the end or fear the start,
Just give your dream a faithful heart.

Within you lives a glowing light,
It leads you forward, bold and bright.

Success is near—just trust your way,
One step, one breath, one gentle day.

Don't be too strict, don't hold too tight,
Let life unfold in its own light.

In a blink, your dreams take flight,

With joy that shines and hearts made right.

When all is sweet and days are new,

I'll stand beside you, loving true.

The Path of the Lost Son

I recall one day,
Lost in my own haze,
Like a swift-footed deer,
I spun in a maze.

The smoke of a cigarette,
Wine in my hand,
I drank until dizzy,
Till I couldn't withstand.

For hours I laughed,
Or suddenly cried,
Shaking and reeling,
No longer I'd hide.

I sang on my way,
Or preached with great zeal,
Calling to the elders,
To the youth, to feel.

I reached home at last,
With pain in the air,
I made the heavens
Taste my despair.

One spat in my path,
With fire in their eyes,
Another compared me
To kin, to my surprise.

The world searched my wet eyes,
Full of woe,
My voice echoed louder
Than donkeys' low.

Before the door,
My lifeless form lay,
A tinge of fear crept in
At the end of the day.

Behind me,
A crooked hand I saw,

Stirring within me
A moment of awe.

A few chips and puffs,
A seed here and there,
I found in my pocket,
Empty and bare.

My drunken face,
No joy to behold,
My mother, the angel,
Her love pure and bold.

She saw me and trembled,
Frozen with dread,
Her innocent flower,
Now grim and dead.

With candy and water,
She tried to restore,
Her tears and sweat
Pulled me to the floor.

I was content in my chaos,

Indifferent, unfazed,

Until my father appeared,

Fury in his gaze.

Like an eagle spotting prey

From afar,

He descended upon me,

A scorned star.

One hand raised high,

The other pressed down,

A foe in his brow,
I felt the weight pound.

His slap, a thunder
That silenced my fears,
All laughter and sorrow
Wiped from my ears.

A flood of comfort
Followed his might,
Like a tiger's embrace,
Clutching so tight.

My body, lifeless,
Pulled like a string,
In the struggle of life,
What did it bring?

His kick left a mark,
A sign of my fate,
Half-deaf to his voice,
I still couldn't relate.

I braced for a blow,
To shatter me free,
Until his wisdom
Swept over me, softly.

He spoke of strength,
Of love, of grace,
Shifting my path
With a tender embrace.

I made a vow
To wear his advice as my crown,
Through my youth and my old age,
Never to drown.

Patience dries up,
Like the almond's oil,
Respect after death?
A forgotten toil.

Recall your childhood,
The tears that you shed—

Did you have no burdens
When sleep left you dead?

Strength rises with age,
But does it remain?
You left home, a wanderer,
Lost in the rain.

Returning like a donkey,
Dancing in pain,
I forgive you once more,
But heed my refrain.

Let reason guide you,
Set boundaries and pace,
For in wisdom's words
Lies a true saving grace.

Like a dagger, his words
Cut deep in my heart,
Shattering folly,
Tearing it apart.

I vowed to stay true,
Till life ebbs away,
To honor my parents,
Come what may.

Their love is sacred,
Their mercy my guide—
On their strength and wisdom,
I will forever rely.

Contrast

It's as simple as playing the piano:

Fingers striking black and white,

Each note to be heard,

Yet completion comes when silence takes flight.

The moon ascends, the sun declines;

The demon roams till dawn's first sign.

Embrace it — the melody unique to your life;
Let silence linger, but let strife come alive.

Touch the unknown without fear;
Let the sky bear witness to every tear.
If the demon wanders near,
Unleash your beast to confront the insincere.

The answers lie within, as silence grows;
Dance with your truth, and watch your wisdom unfold.

**Note: The mood travels like a rollercoaster, rising and falling, dancing with blacks and whites, hearing life's notes, or skipping them — and you wonder why your heart feels untamed. It's all your reflections, your understandings—liking someone or something reflects your conscious self, while disliking them speaks the language of your unconscious mind.*

III. Cultural Transition and Reflection

Moved to Denmark

I recall the day
In April fair,
When first I stepped
On land so bare,

With swiftness, lightness,
Soft yet bold,
Through spring entwined
With snow and cold.

My passport's pages,
White and wide,
Like Karkheh's* stream,
So vast, untied,

Yet hope remained,
My heart was bright—
To see them filled
Felt just so right.

The customs officer,
Gaze so stern,
With doubts that made
My spirit churn,

Once more he asked,
With sharp demand,
"What is your purpose
In this land?"

A moment passed—
Then came my say:
"To seek out wisdom
On my way,

To master knowledge,
Skill, and art,
To play a wise
And noble part."

He raised the stamp,
And with a sound,

Upon my page
It firmly bound,

And so began
My northern quest,
In lands of wind
And endless west.

Their people, fair,
With faces bright,
Their hearts were kind,
Their ways polite,

Each busy in
Their daily stride,
With heads bent low
In rules' abide.

The city shone
In beauty vast,
Yet veiled in hush
That held me fast.

Its people followed
Law so tight—
No heart pursued
What strayed from sight.

Each soul must frame
Their life in bounds,
To earn their bread
And stand their ground.

Yet those whose dreams
Rise high and free
Must mask their thoughts
In secrecy.

Thus passed my first day
In this place,
This northern land,
This foreign space.

So heed these words,
Both old and new—

For wisdom waits

To speak to you.

**Note: Karkheh is a significant river in southwestern Iran, primarily flowing through the Khuzestan province. It originates in the Zagros Mountains and eventually empties into the Shatt al-Arab. The river plays a crucial role in the region's agriculture and irrigation, especially in the fertile plains of Khuzestan. It is also known for its historical significance, as it was once the boundary between ancient Mesopotamia and Persia.*

Copenhagen Dream

One day,
A thought took sudden flight,
And so began
My silent fight.

A quest unknown,
Yet hope held strong—
A distant land
Where I might belong.

My heart, like a bird,
Yearned to flee its cage,
Yet love still warmed
The homebound stage.

I sought a place
Where soul could breathe,
Where waves and silence
Gently wreathe.

To Copenhagen
I sailed with dreams in hand,
Where futures bloom
In northern land.

It was time to root,
To find my space—
A room, a task,
A rightful place.

But rooms were rare,
And doors were closed,
And jobs for skill
Were not disposed.

The days grew thin,
The funds ran dry—
Too proud to beg,
Too starved to lie.

A shrunken belly,
A hollow plea—

No feast, no fire,
Just need in me.

So I found a job
With nothing grand—
To pick and pack
With worn-out hands.

Through sterile halls
I pushed my cart,
With grace and haste
And aching heart.

Speed was praise,
In silence crowned,
In races where
No words were found.

Night bled into day,
The shifts ran long,
Our laughter soft,
But backs stayed strong.

The taxman came

With papered grin,

And left us counting

Crumbs within.

Ah, the West—

So golden from afar,

Yet not built on dreams,

But sweat and scar.

Once we heard

Drums from distant shores,

But now we know
What pride ignores.

So hear me now,
Young hearts that roam:
No crown outshines
The soil of home.

Greed may call
With velvet tone,
But burns the soul
When left alone.

Greed may whisper
With silken breath,
But burns the soul
Like a fire of death.

A Spring in Norway

Once with friends,
We took our flight,
To a land of beauty,
Pure delight.

Its forests deep
And mountains high—
We watched in awe
Beneath the sky.

But when we stepped off
From the ship,
The sky grew dark,
The winds did whip.

A gentle rain
Began to moan,
Then turned to floods
With thunder's tone.

In panic,
Fear within our eyes,
We raised our hands
Up to the skies:

"O Lord above,
We came as friends,
To find some peace,
To make amends.

We've left our homeland
Just for days,
To breathe, to laugh,
In lighter ways.

But now, O Lord,
Please hear our plea,
Protect us from
This raging sea!"

Thus it was—
Springtime in Norway:

One moment calm,
The next astray.

You never know
What comes around—
A flood, the sun,
Or leaves wind-bound.

By night,
We reached a forest inn,
A cozy place,
The fire within.

And while there wasn't
Much to do,
We gathered close,
Our friendships grew.

But then,
As stories filled the air,
Came Mona's voice
With pointed flair:

"Men lack thanks!"
She boldly claimed,
And Linda, too,
Her voice proclaimed.

Each time their words
Began to flare,
My faith with Jawad
Sparked mid-air.

"Our wives," we thought,
"Their hearts seem sore,
And now they speak
Of burdens more."

They counted all
That they had done—
"While you," they said,
"Have barely begun!

We cook, we clean,
We bear the weight,

While you just sit

And call it fate!"

Their words like daggers

Pierced our pride,

Our hearts were bruised—

We stepped aside.

It seemed our efforts,

Though so true,

Meant little
In their point of view.

We said: "Dear ladies,
Young and wise,
Where did such harsh
Demand arise?

All we had,
We gave with grace,
Without complaint,
Without a trace."

"But now," we said,
"Your wants have grown,
Far beyond
The seeds we've sown.

Where is fairness,
Where is praise,
For all we gave
In countless ways?"

If we can't see
The gifts we're shown,
And ask for more
Than we have known,

We blind ourselves
With sheer demand,
And miss the warmth
Within our hand.

We hoped for kindness
From our own—
But maybe that
Was wrongly shown.

So, friend,
I end this verse with care:
Let service be
Without fanfare.

For pain is born
When wants take lead,

And joy comes
When you tend your need.

Live kindly,
Speak with gentle tone,
And praise the gifts
That you are shown.

For those who seek
Just flaws to find—
Will miss the gold
They leave behind.

IV. Mindfulness and Living in the Present

Let it go

Live in the present,
Embrace today,
Don't wait for time
To slip away.

Not ten thousand years
Are yours to keep—
Death walks beside you,
Still and deep.

While life is here,
Within your hands,
Be kind, be good—
Meet its demands.

For time is fleeting,
Passing fast,
The moment now
Is all that lasts.

Let go of plans,
Leave control,

Feel life's essence,
Make it whole.

When last did you,
With focused mind,
Leave the past
And future far behind?

The laughter of my child
So bright,
The sun's warm touch,
The golden light.

True joy is found
In moments small,
Not in the chase
To have it all.

Breathe as if
It were your last—
Not in sorrow—
Let joy hold fast.

Let this be

A call so true,

To live with purpose,

Cherish too.

We're born to die,

So live and see

Where life may lead—

Let answers be.

Accept what comes

With open heart,

And let this moment

Be your start.

All has to change—

Life ebbs and flows,

Embrace the tide,

Let go of woes.

Change is certain,

Let it flow.

Struggles fade,

When we let go.

Mindfulness whispers,

"Always be aware,

Ask yourself daily,

'Am I truly there?'"

Persiansk

The present moment,

All we own—

Yet how it's lost,

How fast it's flown.

Surrender

To live is to yield,
To bow to the stream,
To serve the poor
In midnight's gleam.

In silence of night,
Fall into prayer—
Rise, kneel, or sit
With sacred care.

Let Mary's purity
Be your way,
Let virtue guard
Where shadows sway.

Desire fades
When the soul is still,
This world is a dancer
With a reckless will.

Polish the heart

With a seeker's grace,

And speak with wisdom,

Not endless pace.

The body is crafted

Limb by limb,

But guard the tongue—

It often dims.

Do you know

What makes the noble known?

Respecting all,

In every tone.

Time slips by

Like wind through trees,

So worship now,

Before it flees.

Close your eyes, look within

While the whole world
Spoke of Corona's sting,
I wandered through Verona
In early spring.

The locals stitched lace
With delicate grace,
Marching the main road
At a calm, quiet pace.

But my wife and I,
Bold souls at heart,
Chose gravel and thorns—
A different start.

Full of ourselves,
Lost in youthful delight,
We laughed too loud,
Far out of sight.

We thought it was easy—

No need for might,

A hero would rise,

And all would be right.

But the road climbed high,

Broken and steep,

Our car gave in;

Doubt started to creep.

Lightning cracked
As the heavens roared,
We dashed through the storm,
By chaos floored.

No path ahead,
No way to flee,
Till my mother's voice
Came back to me:

"If trouble strikes
And shadows play,
Close your eyes
And turn away.

Breathe once deep,
Let stillness begin—
No lies, no masks,
Just truth within."

And when hardship falls
And comfort dies,

Close your eyes
And lift your cries.

Pray first for the one
You love the most,
For human hearts
Easily become lost.

The hand that sends
The storm and flame
Is the same that grants
You sight and name.

Pray to Him
While you still have breath,
Before the burdens
Weigh you toward death.

Could we gather unity
In love's true name?
We spoke at length—
Is God for only one to claim?

Who is who,
And what is right?
Show courtesy first,
And shine your light.

Turn kindly toward
Each soul you meet—
It softens anger
And makes grace complete.

Strive for goals
That are noble and true,
Help will come—
Let nonsense undo.

And so at last,
In peace we stayed—
And all our sorrow
Slipped away.

In the Keep of Sorrows

If you fear the fall,
Then leap—
For hidden in falling,
The soul finds release.

Three sorrows
Walk beside our days—
Each one a doorway,
Each one a blaze.

The first is light:
A trial you steer—
With your own hand,
You can change its sphere.

The second strikes
With burning loss—
A loved one gone,
Your weeping the cost.

The third is deepest,
The hardest to bear:
You neither fight,
Nor flee—only stare.

It is the sorrow
That breaks you apart,
Yet leaves behind
The strongest heart.

Rise by night
With a quiet flame,
Holding hope
Where none remains.

If you can heal
What lies in your hand,
You've turned sorrow
Into sacred land.

If not,
Then bear the ache with grace,

And find release

In your own embrace.

Be not a stranger

To those who cared,

Nor pour your pain

Into broken prayers.

For sorrow, too,

Can teach and weave—

And every tear,

A soul's reprieve.

V. Resilience and Inner Strength

The Power of Silence

Oh dear,
It hurts when a loved one betrays—
Whispers behind you,
Setting hearts ablaze.

Yet silence speaks
Louder than any retort—
Walk away with dignity,
Make it your fort.

When they lie,
They crave your reply,
They bait you to battle,
To see you comply.

But engage,
And you're trapped in their twisted game—
Let time and truth
Reveal every name.

The more you defend,
The deeper you're spun—
Words become weapons,
The damage is done.

Stop reacting,
Let karma take lead—
Nature restores,
And the soul is freed.

Betrayal stings,
But it teaches you well—
Where trust has fallen,
Self-respect will swell.

Confront, seek apology—
How will it end?
Or leave in silence,
Let wounds transcend.

Oh yes,
Insults can cut deep inside—

Yet responding
Only feeds their pride.

To be unlike them
Is the finest revenge—
Walk the higher road,
Dignity's pledge.

You ask
Where true power resides?
In detachment,
Where real peace abides.

No second chances,
No desperate plea—
The truth unfolds,
Just wait and see.

One last lesson,
Simple and true:
In stillness lies strength;
In silence, what's true.

Let them mock,

Let them sneer—

Hold your peace,

Stay clear.

Tomorrow without You

If tomorrow must be lived
Without you near,
Then let it be—
There's no need for dawn to appear.

Rain,
Why do you no longer
Wash away my pain?
In thirst,
I lost myself—my very name.

You know well
The depths of my countless despair,
You know every twist and turn,
Each silent prayer.

The candle that burns
In longing sighs with flame—
In your distant sunlight,
Yearning bears no shame.

Cursed be you,
O empty cloud, so bare—

Bring rain to cleanse
My sorrow, if you dare.

The lake of my eyes
Has long since dried—
And now,
My grief has no place to hide.

Everybody Talks

I remember one night—
I slipped away,
Frozen in silence,
My soul stripped of day.

I wandered decades,
Blind and torn,
While voices pierced me,
Proud and worn.

"Do this," they said,
"Or better that way—
Obey the rules,
Or fall astray."

They called me friend,
But saw their own face—
None dared search
For a deeper place.

They boasted wisdom,
Sharp and bright,
Yet crumbled fast
At trial's first bite.

Now I vow—
This silence will end.
I'll challenge each
Self-made saint who pretends.

Unless you've drunk
From sorrow's flame,
Stay silent, friend—
Wild words are lame.

Each time you speak,
Ask what you seek—
Is it truth,
Or the hunger to be unique?

Those taught the secrets,
Whispered deep,

Sealed their lips

And sowed their keep.

V. Resilience and Inner Strength

VI. Love and Longing

Dear Soulmate- Come

O you

Whose tale has no end—

Come.

My heart,

For your gaze,

Did bloom again—

Come.

Across the desert

Of your absence I blew—

In the heart of silence,

Your name broke through—

Come.

Not for my heart,

Nor these tears I weep—

But for your soul's

Own sake, so deep—

Come.

O breeze of dawn

By the beloved's gate—

Kiss the dust

And whisper our fate—

Come.

Without your grace,

My song lies still—

Though I wrote this ghazal*

With no claim or will—

Come.

**Note: The ghazal is a classical poetic form rooted in Persian and Arabic literature, characterized by rhyming couplets and a repeating refrain. It often explores themes of love, loss, and divine longing.*

Stars Falling from Your Gaze

Tonight,
From the heavens of your gaze,
Stars descend
Upon my verse.

In winter's
Barren pages' place,
My pen skis,
Leaving words diverse.

My fevered lines,
In passion's fire,
Scream aloud,
With burnt attire.

Yet once again,
They turn to ash—
Revived by the Phoenix*
In a flash.

New words are born—

Let them soar high,

Let them wander

Freely across the sky.

Let sighs of fire,

Soft and true,

Breathe life into me,

As I seek you.

Do you know
What I long for most?
To be with you alone,
I boast.

If life were granted
A thousand times—
Again and again,
I'd call you home, sublime.

The storm inside me
Swells so wide—
Only your words
Can calm the tide.

So full of you,
I yearn to fade,
To die beneath
Your gentle raid.

Yes, this is love—
Its dawn, its birth,

Though where it leads,
I cannot guess its worth.

But why should endings
Always be sad,
When love is a mystery—
Both good and bad?

**Note: The Phoenix (or "Simurgh" in Persian mythology) is a mythical bird known for its regenerative powers. According to legend, when it grows old, the Phoenix bursts into flames and is reborn from its own ashes. This symbol of renewal and immortality has been a powerful motif in Persian literature and symbolizes the cyclical nature of life, death, and rebirth.*

Thirsty of Your Companion

With all my restless,

Tattered ways,

I chase your smell,

I seek the gaze.

I've come so far

To kiss you on face,

To lose my eyesight

Staring at its blaze.

No borrowed warmth

Can feed my craze—

Only your fire

Can leave me amazed.

I've wandered through deserts,

Lost in a maze,

Seeking a kiss

Through the thickening haze.

You are the fate

I hold most true—

But tell me, love,
Do you know it too?
Speak to me, speak—
It's been too long.
I've thirsted for your voice,
Your endless song.
Where do you lead me,
Love, tonight?
Wherever you go,
As long as I'm in sight.

You are wrong, Ramin

I remember a day—
My wife, distraught,
Came to me like a jackal,
Her fury caught.

Her face, once calm,
Now deeply strained—
My slender cypress bent,
Her beauty waned.

She called me "fool,"
"Ignorant," "blind," and "base"—
I whispered,
My love, your sorrow breaks my grace.

What have I done
To deserve this shame?
Why am I the one
You choose to blame?

She said,

You know nothing—not this, not that.

Each act of yours

A stumbling fall, falling flat.

And so she built

Her fences, brick by brick,

While I fought weary

Through anguish thick.

Each step I took

To bring her peace,

She turned to ice—

And warmth would cease.

"I'm not happy," she said,

"Nor at ease by your side—

There's no way you'll feel

The storm I hide."

Lost in thought,

My sorrow grew—

What is marriage worth

If it cuts you through?

All my kindness

Seemed in vain—

Each seed of love

She saw as stain.

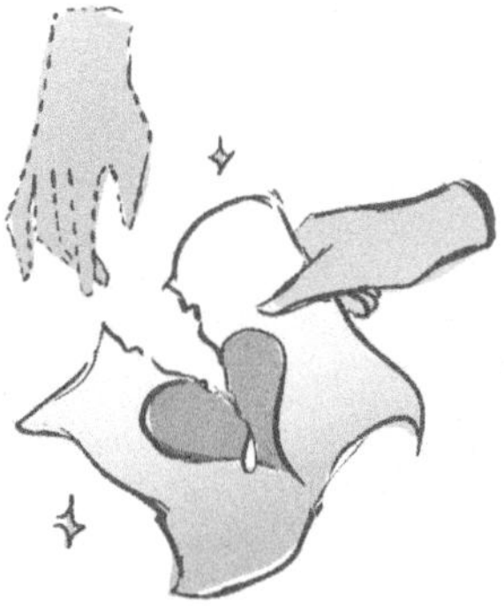

You were meant to be

My soul's own part,

But you strayed too far

From the rhythm of my heart.

Love needs no reason,
No defense—
But you were never present,
Not ever since.

If ever I raised my voice,
It wasn't rage—
But grief that tore me,
Page by page.

You never knew
I burned each night—
Grief's fire
Swallowed all my light.

Come—be kind,
Endure a mile.
I carry wounds
From a younger trial.

My share of earth
Is no more than a grave—

To live while dying—
How long must I stay brave?

Look at the sun—
How free it stays,
Kissing the sea
With morning's rays.

This bittersweet world
Is but a dream—
Death ends it all—
The path's not what it seems.

Forgiveness flows
From love's own stream—
So forgive, and go—
Though tears may redeem.

No Rest

So many trials,
This heart put to the test—
No rest.

Among the crowds,
The soul still seeks its nest—
No rest.

With saints and sages,
I have humbly sat,
Yet even there,
This ache found no rest—
No rest.

A voice inside says,
"Friend, your work is grand,"
Yet still the world
Misreads my quest—
No rest.

I dream of Damavand*,

Its breathless height,

Where Zahhak* writhes beneath,

Suppressed—

No rest.

The pain I hide

Is etched into my chest,

I carry it

As fate's own bequest—

No rest.

I wept at birth,

Then laughed through every breath,

But knew,

Beneath both joy and death—

No rest.

Though love and light

May fill my heart today,

Tomorrow comes,

And steals away—

No rest.

**Mount Damavand: The highest peak in Iran and a symbol of Persian mythology and resilience.*

**Note: Damavand mount/Zahhak (also spelled Zahak or Azhi Dahaka): A tyrannical figure in Persian mythology from Ferdowsi's Shahnameh. He was a tyrant king who was deceived by Ahriman (the devil) and grew serpents on his shoulders that demanded human brains for nourishment. Eventually defeated by the hero Fereydun (a powerful symbol of the triumph of good over evil in Persian lore), Zahhak was imprisoned beneath Mount Damavand, where he remains restless, symbolizing the eternal struggle against evil.*

VII. Spiritual Growth and Inner Peace

Unity

Single, homo, couple-life—none define us,
Not even after life, as we carry our dust.
You once told me, *"Let go of it all,"*
Who knows if we've ventured so far at all?

In pursuit of our essence, let conflicts be borne,
Endure them—for in their fire, we are reborn.
Let go of the ego, and in its place,
All that is needed will find its grace.

They say: *To succeed, focus and commit,*
Yet too much focus may cause us to split.
When facing conflict, don't let anger take hold,
Let go, my dear, and watch life unfold.

No wing can soar if it's tightly restrained,
Release what grips you—and peace will be gained.

The Seeds We Sow

O heart,
Go sit beside the sea,
Where moonlight
Gently lifts from us.

I place my hope
In what is good,
And trust that God
Will shift for us.

The world is fair—
Look well, my friend,
Why darken thought
With needless fear?

Cut evil quickly
At its root,
Or tears shall drift
From us like streams.

If you would spread good
Among all souls,
Then cleanse your deeds
With each new day.

Let guilt be swift
To fall away,
And leave no shadow
On our way.

The breeze ran softly
Through your hair,
The rain kissed both
Your quiet eyes.

You are so full of grace
That even streams
In sorrow
Lift for us.

Come—be the soul's
Sweet peace on earth,

Lift the beggar
When he falls.

Sow not the seeds
Of grief and strife,
Lest fate return
Them back to us.

Fleeting love

One night I set forth,
Alone in my roam,
To drown my sorrows
In a tavern's home.

Exile's sad weight
Was tied to my chest—
I sought to forget,
To drink and find rest.

Two hundred full glasses—
Let wine be my guide.
Whatever may happen,
Let fate now decide.

As I reached for my cup,
Lost deep in thought,
A girl sat beside me—
What fortune I caught!

She smiled and asked,
"From where do you hail?
You don't know my tongue?
You look so frail."

Her gaze found my own,
And my heart lost its way—
Why did all my griefs
Suddenly stray?

I stared and I trembled,
My body felt weak,

My lips longed for hers
But could not speak.

She swayed a little,
Then stepped back with grace,
Leaving me stunned
By the charm of her face.

She whispered,
"You're handsome,
But foreign to me;
No future together—
Our paths won't agree."

I drank another—
Was it the fifth or the tenth?
But her words stayed sharp
At every length.

I had come to the tavern
To bury my pain,
Yet love caught my foot
In its treacherous chain.

What endless despair
This foreign land hides—
No matter the turn,
Misfortune still thrives.

O heart,
Take this lesson,
Simple and bright:
Love starts in ease
But ends in plight.

If exile should lead you
To places unknown,
Choose your companions—
Walk not alone.

If you must walk
Where the elephant keeps,
Build your home strong—
Or be crushed in your sleep.

VIII. The Nowruz Series – A Journey Through the Years

Nowruz 1394*

O Lord,
The year of trial is past—
Its heavy chain undone.

Its mountain peaks,
Its thorns and storms,
Now softened by the sun.

The motherland
Grew tight and cold,
No room for breath or grace.

But You bestowed
A path anew,
And so the course was run.

Once more
I call upon Your name,
Submit to what You will;
In all Your wisdom and decree,
My heart and fate are one.

Like Moses
Cast upon the Nile,
A guest within the wave;

Or fire turned
To gardens cool,
Where once the blaze begun—

By promise made:
That ease will come
When hardship's hour departs.

By mercy shown
To those who failed,
By grace that can't be spun.

By signs You gave,
By sacred times,
By sabbath-born of spring,
Reveal the light,
Awaken minds,
Until the self is none.

Let wisdom bloom
In every soul,
Like trees in early rain,
And grant the bow
Of hearts in prayer
Beneath Your rising sun.

If You have seen
Our humble acts,
Our speech both kind and low,
Then let the weight
Of worship glow—
Its worth by You be won.

Let all the prayers
From parent-lips,
And those who've gone before,
Be carried on
The winds of hope,
Until Your will is done.

** Note: Nowruz years follow the Persian Solar Hijri calendar. For reference, 1394 corresponds to 2015 in the Gregorian calendar.*

Nowruz 1396

O God,

The turning of time—

You ordained for a year anew.

The song of Your nightingale

Disturbed the slumber

Of the drunken few.

We cried and lamented,

Seeking to drive away our pain.

Alas, whatever comes is a gift—

But when do we its worth retain?

You decreed

That loss may come

In wealth and health alike,

Yet glad tidings are for the patient—

Of this, the tales strike.

Truly I say,

Every trial

Holds a glimpse
Of knowing You.

Let me say it louder—
That moment of understanding
Is pure and true.

"Waking early and a clear voice"—
Let these be
This year's sign of Eid*.

My prayer for the year:
A beautiful mind,
And Your love
In every prayer and deed.

"Caring for others"
Brings abundance
To the servant's share.

So fill every home's table with joy,
With laughter in the air.

**Eid: Persian New Year celebration marking spring in Iranian tradition.*

Nowruz 1397

O God, as You spin
The thread of our fleeting years,
The veil of ignorance
Has blinded the world with tears.

In the cellar of this world,
So fickle and unkind,
Our hearts we confined,
And left compassion behind.

In pride and self-deceit,
We surged with hungry pace,
Your mercy turned away—
We lost its gentle face.

Trees of cunning rose,
In their disgrace, sky-high,
We reached for worldly crowns,
And let Your grace pass by.

For knowledge, wealth, and name,
We wandered far and wide,
Yet cast away old visas,
Stamped with truths we denied.

O God, our faith is clear—
Monotheism, love, and grace,
To shed all pride and ego,
And seek Your warm embrace.

So see it well, we ask,
Remove illusion's shawl,
Let us drink the wine of service,
And heed Your sacred call.

Ease the path we're on,
Let hearts be born anew,
O God, in every breath,
Let us be true to You.

Nowruz 1399

O friend,
The sight of your face
Brings only tears
To others' eyes.

Through years and months,
Through days and nights,
Our gaze on you
Never dies.

A hundred sorrows
Have clothed the skies,
With pain upon our land,
While poverty's furnace
Burns the joy
From bodies—
Taking what was once so grand.

Perhaps in error,
We wandered paths

That led us
To the depths below.

Yet You are God,
Who welcomes repentance—
Let us not fall low.

We wandered,
And we wander still;
In roaming,
Grant us prayer.

And for all broken hearts
This year,
Keep the wicked
Far from our air.

Nowruz 1401

O Lord,
To You my heart is true—
No wish or loyalty
Is truer than You.

The door of fortune,
Sweet and wide,
Opens at prayer's
Blessed tide.

Do not ask
Of my state, my soul,
For winter's chill
Has taken its toll.

My day begins anew
With light,
A breeze as sweet
As amber bright.

Open my eyes,
Though sad they be—
Let the wheel of fate
Turn free.

Not all who seek
The heart of love
Are worthy of
What stars have above.

The one who understands
The sky
Will rise and reach
The heavens high.

If both bodies
Are stung
By the scorpion's sting,
They'll wander lost
With no place to cling.

O Lord,
Mercy to the thirsty eyes,

Rest the forsaken,

Lift their cries.

For years we've wandered,

Worn and torn—

Through the world,

Weary and worn.

Look now, O Scorpion*,

To the age ahead—

Turn your gaze

Where the new dawn is spread.

**Note: In astrology, the Scorpion (or Scorpio) is often associated with intense transformation, mystery, and deep emotional insight. It is ruled by the planet Pluto, symbolizing power, death, and rebirth. The reference to "the Scorpion" in the poem can be understood as a metaphor for the current age under the astrological influence of Scorpio, believed to be a time marked by emotional intensity, transformation, and profound change. The Scorpion's sting signifies pain and awakening, suggesting that those who endure hardships (the sting) may emerge stronger, with a deeper understanding of life's truths. It also represents the challenges and trials that one must face during this transformative period in time. The reference to "look now, O Scorpion, to the age ahead" alludes to a future shaped by these powerful, sometimes tumultuous energies.*

Nowruz 1402

Two years have passed,
A thousand gone.
Four hundred left,
A secret song.

The omens unfold,
Seven in line—
A feast awaits,
In silence, divine.

Do you not see
The hour draws near,
When truth will shine,
Both pure and clear?

O world, in ruins,
Blind no more,
For truth will open
Every door.

The distant church
Shall soon be gone,
And wisdom's counsel
Overthrown.

In battle's haze,
The weak may fall,
Seeking Eden*,
Answering the call.

Guide your heart
With love, sincere—
With effort,
Your soul will persevere.

Deceit may come,
But kindness will rise,
And mercy rests
Where wisdom lies.

Time flies swift,

A fleeting breeze—

The end approaches,

None to appease.

Our faces bare,

Truth's sweet embrace—

Proof of its power

Upon each face.

I journeyed through realms,

Seeking peace—

A place of order,
Where pain would cease.

But only desolation
Met my eyes—
A world adrift
Beneath the skies.

I wish this sorrow
Were but a dream,
This turmoil, this ache,
A passing beam.

I long to find joy
In a fair face—
Not in shadows,
But truth's embrace.

**Note: Eden: In many religious and mythological traditions, the Garden of Eden is a paradisiacal place where humanity's journey begins. In the Abrahamic faiths, it is described as the original home of Adam and Eve, symbolizing innocence, beauty, and harmony with nature before the fall from grace. The garden represents purity, divine creation, and the ideal state of existence. However, after the fall, it becomes a symbol of loss, exile, and the yearning for spiritual return. In this context, the mention of "Eden" within the poem serves as both a literal and metaphorical longing for a return to a state of peace, purity, and wholeness amidst the struggles and turmoil of life.*

Nowruz 1403

Humor and crude words,
And speech so low,
Must fall beneath—
If God's love you know.

When thoughts of man
Take the wrong path,
The purest nature
Is defiled by their wrath.

If food and wine
Are spread upon your feast,
Let speech be gentle—
For all these are least in joy.

The wheel of fate
Turns, ever in motion,
And who turns their eyes
Finds joy in devotion.

When youth's days arrive,
With strength and grace,
Do not be harsh,
Nor raise your voice in haste.

Look to the young and the old,
To their strife—
One may rise with kindness,
The other with life.

Another spring is near,
And blooms seek the light.
Your heart should grow green,
For it's the divine New Year's sight.

In the dawn's quiet sleep,
Do not be more vain.
With each breath, cleanse,
And work with aim.

Enter the serpent's path,
For good fortune is near,

And let fire burn
What from grace is unclear.

Like the calm gazelle,
Whose fate is set—
Let your body sink in the mud,
If the path is yet.

The final word,
Though told by another's tongue—
I say it's true,
For its wisdom's never unsung.

Sit in my eyes,
O one who is more than me—
That I may show the moon,
Brighter than thee.

Nowruz 1404

Year upon year passed,
And times grew hard.
The enemy's hatred deepened,
His deceit spread far.

This winter, too, departed,
Yet cruelty prevailed.
All the good we spun—
Suddenly, it unraveled, frail.

The pure divine essence,
Once flowing like a living stream,
Through the cycles of years,
Turned from Karkheh to Karun's* dream.

I have no will to question,
For my anger still remains—
As if, at last, God slumbers
Till summer's peak reigns.

This spring has come,
Its end marking autumn's retreat.
Our sorrowful state
Shall not forever repeat.

Rise, let us offer
A prayer at dawn's first light—
For no balm soothes pain
Like whispered praise in delight.

O Lord, the year that passed
Left ruins in the heart—
Rebuild its bricks and fields
Before all falls apart.

We have lamented time,
Our complaints vast and wide—
Yet You, who know my burdens,
Will stand by my side.

With myself, I vowed—
No weapon shall I wield.

For all that comes is good,

If You are the hand that heals.

**Note: Karun River is the longest river in Iran, flowing through the southwestern part of the country, mainly in Khuzestan province. It originates from the Zagros Mountains and is crucial for agriculture, transportation, and hydroelectric power generation in the region. It is also historically significant and has been a key river in the development of ancient civilizations in the area.*

IX. Poetic Meditations

A final hush in the book's rhythm—these distilled verses offer flashes of insight, fragments of spirit, and quiet companions for the reader's own reflection.

About enemies bring complaints to a friend,

But if the friend is the enemy, where shall we go to end?

With an axe on my shoulder, I wander in search,

To break this "worthless" rogue, lost in his own lurch.

To truly see is the essence of being human,

Do not seek faults in others, for that's not the way of the wise.

I vowed to cease speaking of our painful parting,

Yet what can this heart, so prone to breaking,

do with the grief of your love, still departing?

Live in a way that when you die, you soar,

Not in a way that leaves you lost, ignored.

The sleeper knows not the pain of The awake,

Until your own sorrow strikes, you'll never feel
another's ache.

I wish my friend would point out my flaws,

Like a mirror, face to face, with no pause.

Not like a comb, with a thousand tongues,

Speaking behind my back, hair by hair, it stuns.

I began with you, to reach the end of the line,

I left the alley, hoping to find the main road, divine.

If you entangle me, I find joy in my plight,

If you are the cure for my pain, I'm content in my illness' night.

As long as reaching you is still within sight,

Life is a beautiful pain that flows in the night.

It feels like someone within me seeks to deny,

Someone like me, longing to meet my eye.

When sorrow exceeds its bounds, the heart feels old,

The pain of each person measures their age untold.

Life is a flowing stream, it passes by,

Whatever fate awaits us, that will pass, no matter why.

Night arrived, and with it, the day took flight,

My sweet companion stayed with me, through the night.

Her hair like ropes of silk danced in the air,

Her languid eyes, to my heart, did share their care.

The pain struck hard, my rival's heart did break,

An eternal vow, with me, she chose to make.

Acknowledgments

Writing this collection has been both a deeply personal journey and a shared experience, shaped by the love, support, and encouragement of those closest to me.

To my wife, Linda — thank you for your boundless curiosity and the beautiful way you question everything. Your perspective has challenged me to see life through new lenses, to think deeper, and to write with greater honesty. In moments of doubt, your quiet strength carried me. Without you, these poems would not exist.

To my mother, Mehri, whose unconditional love has quietly nurtured the roots of this book — thank you for preserving every piece of my writing, whether born of joy or struggle. I still remember how you saved each poem I wrote during Nowruz or in moments of inner turmoil, capturing them in photos or writing them down when I couldn't. This collection lives because you believed it was worth preserving. Half of these poems found their way back to me because you kept them safe.

To my sister, Maryam, whose sharp insight and unshakable belief in me have pushed me forward time and again — thank you. You championed my first little booklet, even when it felt like a failure, and you never let me give up. This book is the result of the resilience you helped ignite.

To my father, Ebrahim — thank you for your great sense of humor, which has been a guiding light through life's challenges. Your unwavering commitment to your work and family has shaped me more deeply than words can capture. The traits I carry, the persistence I hold to, are a mirror of your example, and I am endlessly grateful for that inheritance.

To my brother, Abdulrahman — thank you for always having my back, in ways both visible and unseen. You supported me when I moved to Denmark, you stood by me in my teenage years when life's shadows loomed, even shielding me from danger when needed. You have been not only a brother but a role model whose decisions, sacrifices, and wisdom have shaped my path. So much of whatever I have achieved carries your fingerprints.

To the poetry community — both online and in real life — thank you for being a space where words can breathe, evolve, and find meaning. To the poets who came before me, whose verses lit a fire in me, and to the editors who lent their time and care to sharpen mine — I am deeply grateful.

And finally, to you — the reader. Thank you for picking up this book, for making space in your life for these words. My deepest hope is that somewhere in these pages, you find echoes of your own story, and a moment of stillness or clarity that stays with you long after the last line.

About the Author

Ramin Taheri was born in May 1987 in Shiraz, Iran—a city steeped in poetic tradition and home to literary legends like Hafez and Saadi. From an early age, he found himself drawn to the beauty of language and the depth of the classical Persian *Ghazal*, with its timeless meditations on love, longing, and the divine.

Although his professional path led him into the world of engineering, Ramin has never strayed far from poetry. Writing has remained his sanctuary—a way to process the complexities of love, loss, identity, and the meaning of existence. His work often weaves together personal reflection with spiritual exploration, revealing a mind constantly in search of deeper truths.

In 2016, Ramin moved to Denmark, beginning a new chapter of his life that brought with it the gifts of marriage and fatherhood. Today, he works as an Engineer in Denmark.

A lover of languages, Ramin speaks Persian, English, Danish, and German. Off the page, Ramin finds joy in the rhythm of football, which he sees not just as a sport, but as a dance of coordination and freedom. Gardening offers him moments of solitude and grounding—whether it's cutting grass, watering flowers, or simply feeling the earth with his hands. At home, he introduced his family to Persian cuisine, though it's now his wife who has mastered the art, filling their kitchen with the vibrant aromas of saffron and spices.

Persiansk is his most intimate collection to date—a poetic journey through the seasons of the soul, shaped over the years and including reflections from Nowruz 1394 to 1404. With a voice that bridges cultures and emotions, Ramin invites readers into a world where poetry becomes a mirror, a refuge, and a way forward.

Social media:

Instagram: *@persiansk2020*

Email: *persiansk2020@gmail.com*

Thank you for sharing this journey.

Made in the USA
Las Vegas, NV
25 June 2025

24050624R00100